this prayer journal belongs to

....

....

DATE

*I will lift up my eyes to
the mountains; from where
shall my help come? My help
comes from the LORD, who
made heaven and earth.*

PSALM 121:1-2

Unless otherwise indicated, all Scripture quotations are taken from the New American Standard Bible®, © 1960, 1962, 1963, 1968, 1971, 1972, 1973, 1975, 1977, 1995 by The Lockman Foundation. Used by permission. (www.Lockman.org)

Verses marked NLT are taken from the *Holy Bible*, New Living Translation, copyright © 1996, 2004, 2007, 2013 by Tyndale House Foundation. Used by permission of Tyndale House Publishers, Inc., Carol Stream, Illinois 60188. All rights reserved.

Cover by Connie Gabbert Design + Illustration

Interior design by Janelle Coury

Published in association with William K. Jensen Literary Agency, 119 Bampton Court, Eugene, Oregon 97404

PRAYERS OF MY HEART

Copyright © 2018 by Debbie Taylor Williams
Published by Harvest House Publishers
Eugene, Oregon 97408
www.harvesthousepublishers.com

ISBN 978-0-7369-7397-7

Printed in China

HARVEST HOUSE PUBLISHERS
EUGENE, OREGON

18 19 20 21 22 23 24 25 26 / RDS-JC / 10 9 8 7 6 5 4 3 2 1

Welcome

Most people want to pray. As a matter of fact, studies show that most people do pray.[1] Prayer is a powerful blessing. It's the means by which we enter into communion with God. The Bible teaches us that God hears our prayers (Psalm 65:2) and responds according to His name (John 14:13–14). Prayer has challenges, though. Which of the following have you experienced?

- You promise, "I'll pray for you," and then forget.
- You shoot "arrow" prayers to God but don't spend quality time in prayer.
- Your mind wanders when you pray.
- You have prayer time but seem to repeat the same words.
- You don't hear Him directing you the way He seems to do for others.

I've struggled with all of the above. One that especially bothered me was when I'd forget to pray for someone who asked for prayer. Several years ago, in an attempt to find a concise way to record prayer requests, I developed the column-based prayer chart in this journal. It was an answer to prayer because I'd been searching for a way to keep up with prayer needs for my family, my friends, my church, my ministry, the unsaved, and our nation.

But first, why journal? Are there any benefits?

---

1 Aaron Cline Hanbury, "Research: Most Americans Pray Every Day, and Other Facts About Prayer in America," *Relevant*, May 4, 2017, https://relevantmagazine.com/slice/research-most-americans-pray-every-day/.

Seven Benefits to Journaling

1. *Journaling increases your intimacy with God.* Arrow prayers are good. However, if my husband and I only visited for brief moments or when multitasking, we wouldn't have the intimate relationship we enjoy. Second Chronicles 16:9 says, "The eyes of the Lord search the whole earth in order to strengthen those whose hearts are fully committed to him" (NLT). When we make time to be alone with God with our Bible, journal, and pen in hand, He notices.

2. *Journaling increases your focus and concentration, making your prayer time more productive and effective.* In the "Week at a Glance" section, you'll record the names of those for whom you pray on a regular basis. As you move your pen from one column to the next, your mind will focus on each person's prayer need. Instead of wasting time because of a wandering mind, you'll spend profitable time in focused prayer.

3. *Journaling renews your mind.* "When we write something down, research suggests that as far as our brain is concerned, it's as if we were doing that thing. Writing seems to act as a kind of mini-rehearsal for doing."[2] When we prayerfully write, "Stand firm against the schemes of the devil," those words signal to our brain, "This is important." When we journal according to Scripture, that act renews our mind.

4. *Journaling helps build your memory, mindfulness, and faith.* When you write, it's as if you're writing the words in your memory. You'll find blank journaling pages at the back of the book. Use them to begin your prayer time in worship of God. Think about His nature in relation to your life as you prayerfully write His name in praise. Write "Thank You!" or "Praise You!" beside answered prayers. Doing so increases your knowledge of God, builds memories of His faithfulness, and makes you more mindful of Him.

5. *Journaling increases your overall well-being.* Reports show that people who

---

2 Dustin Wax, "Writing and Remembering: Why We Remember What We Write," *Lifehack*, http://www.life hack.org/articles/featured/writing-and-remembering-why-we-remember-what-we-write.html.

keep a gratitude journal are more optimistic than those who don't.[3] When we let our heart and pen flow with words of praise, answered prayers, confessions, and forgiveness, we're not merely more optimistic.[4] Studies show that optimism improves our physical and mental fitness.[5]

6. Journaling tunes your ears to God's voice. In Isaiah 55:3, the Lord says, "Incline your ear and come to Me. Listen, that you may live." When you kneel or sit before God with journal and pen in hand, you are, in effect, lifting up your soul for Him to speak to you (Psalm 130:6). This is one of the biggest blessings of journaling. In silence and stillness, we open our hearts for His Spirit to fill us. We open our ears to listen to Him.

7. Journaling adds clarity and insight into your relationship with God. Do you ever have jumbled, mixed, or unclear thoughts? Studies show that "writing helps you see your thoughts on paper. It adds clarity to what you're thinking."[6]

For instance, we may not realize we feel hopeless until we prayerfully write, "Increase hope." We may think we've put bitterness aside until we journal God's attribute: "Merciful." Our journal reflects our thoughts back to us. Our prayers reflect what God sees in our heart, which is important if want to love Him with all our heart and effectively intercede for others.

Two Benefits of Column-Based Prayer Journaling

1. Journaling in a column under a person's name eliminates the need to rerecord repeated requests.

2. Answered prayers are easy to find under a person's name. Highlighting or dating answers is a celebratory faith builder.

3 Harvard Health Publishing, *Healthbeat*, "Giving Thanks Can Make You Happier," https://www.health.harvard.edu/healthbeat/giving-thanks-can-make-you-happier.

4 Ibid.

5 Harvard Health Publishing, *Harvard Men's Health Watch*, "Optimism and Your Health," May 2008, https://www.health.harvard.edu/heart-health/optimism-and-your-health.

6 Dr. Caroline Leaf, *Switch on Your Brain* (Grand Rapids, MI: Baker Books, 2013), 181.

Three Formats in One Journal

On the following pages, you'll find three different sections to help you in your prayer journey. Two are column based, and the third allows room for longer prayers, notes, and meditations. You can use one section or all three.

Month at a Glance

Let's look at the "Month at a Glance" sample. When people call with prayer requests for surgery, a job interview, or a test, you can easily record prayer prompts. Only a few words are necessary: "John—surgery," "Amber—test." I also use it as a keepsake for birthdays, special events, and milestones. It's a blessing to look back through years of journals and have a memorial that won't crash like an electronic journal might.

Week at a Glance

The "Week at a Glance" is where you write the names of those for whom you pray regularly at the top of each column. Under the columns, you record prayer requests. In the sample, you'll see I label my first column heading "Lord" so I can daily record an attribute for which I praise Him. I often use an attribute of God as a springboard for my prayers.

Under each of the column headings, record your prayer in brief, abbreviated words.

One friend calls her family every Sunday and asks how she can pray for them. They now anticipate her call and look forward to sharing their prayer requests.

Under the "Friends" column, you can ignore the days of the week and use the column to list your friends' prayers. It's a sweet privilege to pray for strength in marriages, guidance in raising children, provision for financial needs, patience in the home, and growth in the Lord.

The "Church/Ministry" column provides a place to record prayers for your ministry events, outreach opportunities, and the Spirit's anointing on pastors and teachers. Or you can designate the column for your life group or Bible study group's prayer requests.

The "USA/Unsaved" column is where you can record requests for the unsaved, our nation, and our leaders.

Meditations, Notes, and Prayers

In this section of your journal, you'll find lined pages. Some of my most precious moments are in stillness before the Father. With pen in hand and Bible and journal open, I record words of worship and confession. I record ministry ideas and "to-dos" the Lord impresses on my heart. I journal Bible verses and sometimes illustrate them to more deeply plant them in my heart. The joy of intimacy with the Savior is abundant!

INSPIRATION

Prayer journaling, for me, is inspirational! Prayer is not just about pouring out our requests to God. Prayer is also about God pouring His will into us. Many times I kneel with my Bible and prayer journal open, not knowing how to pray. But in those moments of silence, the Holy Spirit brings to mind direction and insight. In those moments prayer is dynamic and didactic. It's two-way communion with the Father. On the paper you see only words, but in lives you see change as the dynamic Spirit of God moves in answer to prayer on behalf of His children and kingdom.

A TOOL IN THE MASTER'S HANDS

Prayers of My Heart is a tool to help you pray and then celebrate God's answers. A tool that in our Father's hands can bring forth much fruit. I pray as you make intentional time to be with our living, eternal Lord and Savior that you will discover increased intimacy and joy with Him.

In Christ's joy,

Debbie

Sample Month

SUNDAY	MONDAY	TUESDAY
Marcus – Salvation		Tess – travel safety
Jack substitute teaching – God's anointing	Madison – 1st day of 1st grade	See You at the Pole
Life Group lunch		Jackson – MRI
Whitmans here	Bible study begins	MOPs
Church musical		Dad – birthday

Call upon Me in the day of trouble; I shall rescue you, and you will honor Me.

PSALM 50:15

WEDNESDAY	THURSDAY	FRIDAY	SATURDAY
Women's Bible study			Date Night!
	Volunteer at hospital		3pm Campbell's birthday party
John – surgery		Whitmans here – travel safety	Whitmans here
Praise Team rehearsal	Missy – cancer treatment	Austin & Sara engaged!	Ashton – going away party

	Lord	Spouse	Self	Child
SUNDAY	Almighty Gen 17:1-2	Empower	Fill; walk by Your Spirit	G & C come to know You @ early age
MONDAY	Abides Forever Ps 9:7			
TUESDAY	Able Rom 4:21	Use as Your light	Encourage M in her Ch walk	
WEDNESDAY	Abolisher of Death 2 Tim 1:10	Anoint preparation for Sunday		Kids love Your Word & ways
THURSDAY	Above All Eph 1:21	Witness to Paul	Finish preparation for Conf	
FRIDAY	Adequate 2 Cor 3:5		Anoint speaking/ conference	
SATURDAY	Advocate 1 Jn 2:1	Rest	Women enc & equipped	Develop Christian friends

Child	Family	Friends	Church/Ministry	USA/Unsaved
New friends, R & J visit church	Strengthen P & J with truth		Anoint pastors, teachers	Repent & return to You
		D & S - Sign up marriage course		
	Maggie - be a witness at work	Austin - guide to Your job for him	Moms encouraged at MOPS	Draw unbelievers to You
Kids love Your Word & ways	JJ find job - THANK YOU, LORD!	D & S - reconcile		
	Kirsten - successful rehab	M & K - wise to enemies' schemes	Increased passion for the unsaved	
	Guide A how to deal w/M	Amber - quick recovery	Youth retreat - salvations	Comfort those suffering fr/ hurricanes
Travel safety	JJ's move - safety on road	Bless N & B's wedding		

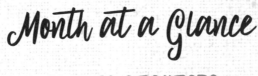

Month at a Glance

PRAYER REQUESTS

*The LORD is near to
all who call upon Him,
to all who call upon Him in truth.*

PSALM 145:18

January

O Lord,
I call upon You;
hasten to me!
Give ear to my
voice when
I call to You!
May my prayer
be counted
as incense
before You;
the lifting up of
my hands as the
evening offering.

Psalm 141:1-2

SUNDAY	MONDAY	TUESDAY

WEDNESDAY	THURSDAY	FRIDAY	SATURDAY

February

I love the LORD, because He hears my voice and my supplications.

PSALM 116:1

SUNDAY	MONDAY	TUESDAY

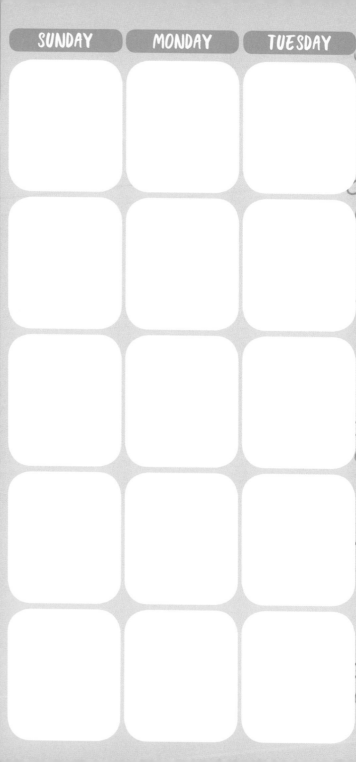

WEDNESDAY	THURSDAY	FRIDAY	SATURDAY

March

SUNDAY	MONDAY	TUESDAY

In my trouble I cried to the LORD, and He answered me.

PSALM 120:1

WEDNESDAY	THURSDAY	FRIDAY	SATURDAY

April

SUNDAY | MONDAY | TUESDAY

I will say to the LORD, "My refuge and my fortress, my God, in whom I trust!"

PSALM 91:2

May

SUNDAY	MONDAY	TUESDAY

The LORD hears the needy and does not despise His who are prisoners.

PSALM 69:33

WEDNESDAY	THURSDAY	FRIDAY	SATURDAY

June

SUNDAY	MONDAY	TUESDAY

Be gracious to me, O God, according to Your lovingkindness; according to the greatness of Your compassion blot out my transgressions.

PSALM 51:1

WEDNESDAY	THURSDAY	FRIDAY	SATURDAY

July

SUNDAY	MONDAY	TUESDAY

Wash me thoroughly from my iniquity and cleanse me from my sin. For I know my transgressions, and my sin is ever before me.

PSALM 51:2-3

WEDNESDAY	THURSDAY	FRIDAY	SATURDAY

August

SUNDAY	MONDAY	TUESDAY

My soul waits for the Lord more than the watchmen for the morning; indeed, more than the watchmen for the morning.

PSALM 130:6

WEDNESDAY	THURSDAY	FRIDAY	SATURDAY

September

SUNDAY	MONDAY	TUESDAY

In my distress I called upon the LORD, and cried to my God for help; He heard my voice out of His temple, and my cry for help before Him came into His ears.

PSALM 18:6

WEDNESDAY	THURSDAY	FRIDAY	SATURDAY

October

SUNDAY	MONDAY	TUESDAY

If I regard wickedness in my heart, the Lord will not hear; but certainly God has heard; He has given heed to the voice of my prayer.

PSALM 66:18-19

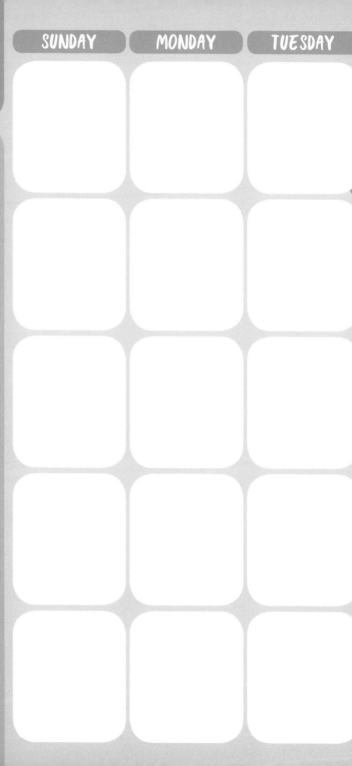

November

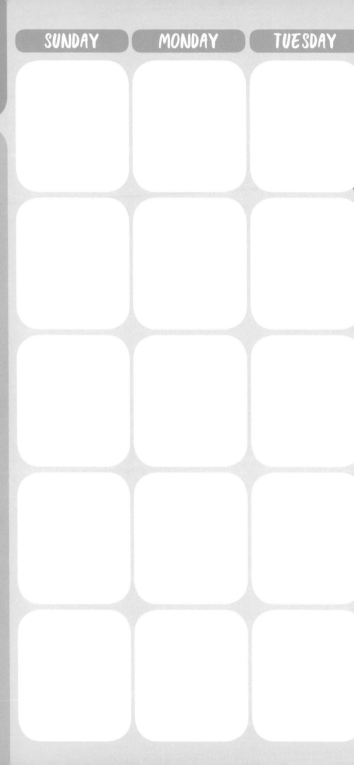

SUNDAY	MONDAY	TUESDAY

WEDNESDAY	THURSDAY	FRIDAY	SATURDAY

December

SUNDAY	MONDAY	TUESDAY

*Every day
I will bless You,
and I will praise
Your name
forever and
ever.*

PSALM 145:2

WEDNESDAY	THURSDAY	FRIDAY	SATURDAY

Week at a Glance

PRAYER REQUESTS

With all prayer and petition
pray at all times in the Spirit,
and with this in view, be on the
alert with all perseverance and
petition for all the saints.

EPHESIANS 6:18

Week OF

_____

SUNDAY

MONDAY

TUESDAY

WEDNESDAY

THURSDAY

FRIDAY

SATURDAY

I say to you, ask, and it will be given to you; seek, and you will find; knock, and it will be opened to you.

LUKE 11:9

Week OF

_____

	SUNDAY	MONDAY	TUESDAY	WEDNESDAY	THURSDAY	FRIDAY	SATURDAY

Week of

___

It will also come to pass that before they call, I will answer; and while they are still speaking, I will hear.

ISAIAH 65:24

SUNDAY	MONDAY	TUESDAY	WEDNESDAY	THURSDAY	FRIDAY	SATURDAY

Week of

_____

Call to Me and I will answer you, and I will tell you great and mighty things, which you do not know.

JEREMIAH 33:3

SUNDAY			
MONDAY			
TUESDAY			
WEDNESDAY			
THURSDAY			
FRIDAY			
SATURDAY			

If you abide in Me, and My words abide in you, ask whatever you wish, and it will be done for you.

JOHN 15:7

SUNDAY

MONDAY

TUESDAY

WEDNESDAY

THURSDAY

FRIDAY

SATURDAY

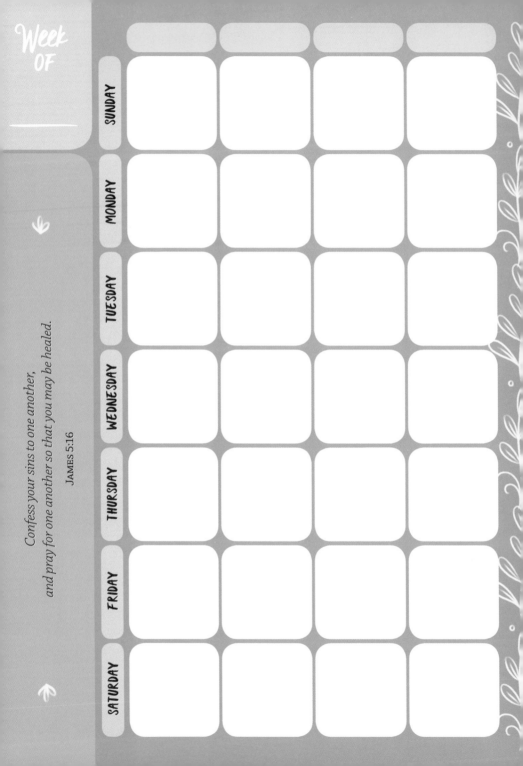

Week of
_____

Confess your sins to one another, and pray for one another so that you may be healed.
James 5:16

SUNDAY

MONDAY

TUESDAY

WEDNESDAY

THURSDAY

FRIDAY

SATURDAY

Week OF

_____

SUNDAY

MONDAY

TUESDAY

WEDNESDAY

THURSDAY

FRIDAY

SATURDAY

You will seek Me and find Me when you search for Me with all your heart.

JEREMIAH 29:13

Week OF

My flesh and my heart may fail,
but God is the strength of my heart and my portion forever.

PSALM 73:26

SUNDAY	MONDAY	TUESDAY	WEDNESDAY	THURSDAY	FRIDAY	SATURDAY

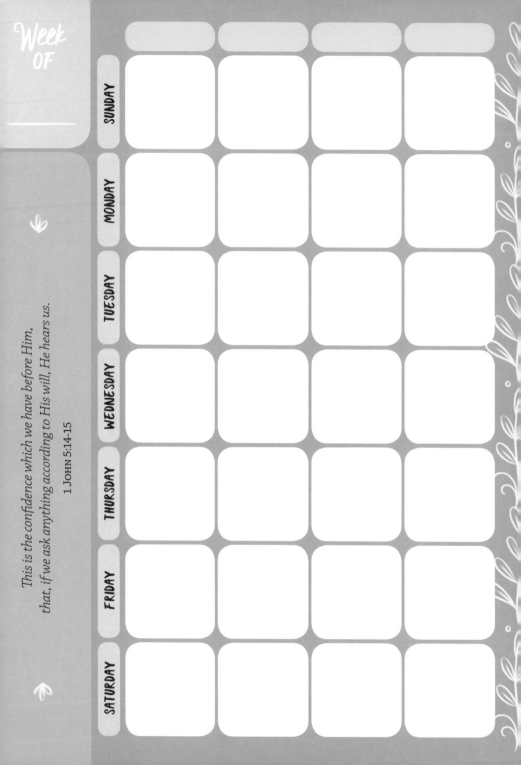

Week OF

_____

This is the confidence which we have before Him, that, if we ask anything according to His will, He hears us.

1 JOHN 5:14-15

SUNDAY

MONDAY

TUESDAY

WEDNESDAY

THURSDAY

FRIDAY

SATURDAY

Week OF

_____

↓

The righteous cry, and the LORD hears and delivers them out of all their troubles.

PSALM 34:17

↑

SUNDAY	MONDAY	TUESDAY	WEDNESDAY	THURSDAY	FRIDAY	SATURDAY

Week OF

_____

On God my salvation and my glory rest;
the rock of my strength, my refuge is in God.

PSALM 62:7

SUNDAY	MONDAY	TUESDAY	WEDNESDAY	THURSDAY	FRIDAY	SATURDAY

The LORD is far from the wicked,
but He hears the prayer of the righteous.

PROVERBS 15:29

	SUNDAY	MONDAY	TUESDAY	WEDNESDAY	THURSDAY	FRIDAY	SATURDAY

Week OF

_____

As for me, I will watch expectantly for the LORD;
I will wait for the God of my salvation.

MICAH 7:7

SUNDAY

MONDAY

TUESDAY

WEDNESDAY

THURSDAY

FRIDAY

SATURDAY

Week OF

_____

In the same way the Spirit also helps our weakness; for we do not know how to pray as we should, but the Spirit Himself intercedes for us with groanings too deep for words.

ROMANS 8:26

	SUNDAY	MONDAY	TUESDAY	WEDNESDAY	THURSDAY	FRIDAY	SATURDAY

Week
OF

_____

When you are praying, do not use meaningless repetition as the Gentiles do, for they suppose that they will be heard for their many words.

MATTHEW 6:7

SUNDAY

MONDAY

TUESDAY

WEDNESDAY

THURSDAY

FRIDAY

SATURDAY

Week OF

_____

In God I have put my trust, I shall not be afraid. What can man do to me?

PSALM 56:11

SUNDAY	MONDAY	TUESDAY	WEDNESDAY	THURSDAY	FRIDAY	SATURDAY

Week OF

_____

	SUNDAY	MONDAY	TUESDAY	WEDNESDAY	THURSDAY	FRIDAY	SATURDAY

Week of

_____

Pray without ceasing.
1 THESSALONIANS 5:17

	SUNDAY	MONDAY	TUESDAY	WEDNESDAY	THURSDAY	FRIDAY	SATURDAY

Week of

_____

When you pray, go into your inner room, close your door and pray to your Father who is in secret, and your Father who sees what is done in secret will reward you.

MATTHEW 6:6

SUNDAY	MONDAY	TUESDAY	WEDNESDAY	THURSDAY	FRIDAY	SATURDAY

*Until now you have asked for nothing in My name;
ask and you will receive, so that your joy may be made full.*

JOHN 16:24

SUNDAY	MONDAY	TUESDAY	WEDNESDAY	THURSDAY	FRIDAY	SATURDAY

Week
OF

_____

My God will supply all your needs according to
His riches in glory in Christ Jesus.

PHILIPPIANS 4:19

	SUNDAY	MONDAY	TUESDAY	WEDNESDAY	THURSDAY	FRIDAY	SATURDAY

Week OF

_____

SUNDAY

MONDAY

TUESDAY

WEDNESDAY

THURSDAY

FRIDAY

SATURDAY

All things you ask in prayer, believing, you will receive.

MATTHEW 21:22

Week OF

_____

SUNDAY

MONDAY

TUESDAY

WEDNESDAY

THURSDAY

FRIDAY

SATURDAY

If two of you agree on earth about anything that they may ask, it shall be done for them by My Father who is in heaven.

MATTHEW 18:19

Week of

_____

With all prayer and petition pray at all times in the Spirit, and with this in view, be on the alert with all perseverance and petition for all the saints.

EPHESIANS 6:18

	SUNDAY	MONDAY	TUESDAY	WEDNESDAY	THURSDAY	FRIDAY	SATURDAY

Week
OF
_____

Devote yourselves to prayer,
keeping alert in it with an attitude of thanksgiving.

COLOSSIANS 4:2

SUNDAY			
MONDAY			
TUESDAY			
WEDNESDAY			
THURSDAY			
FRIDAY			
SATURDAY			

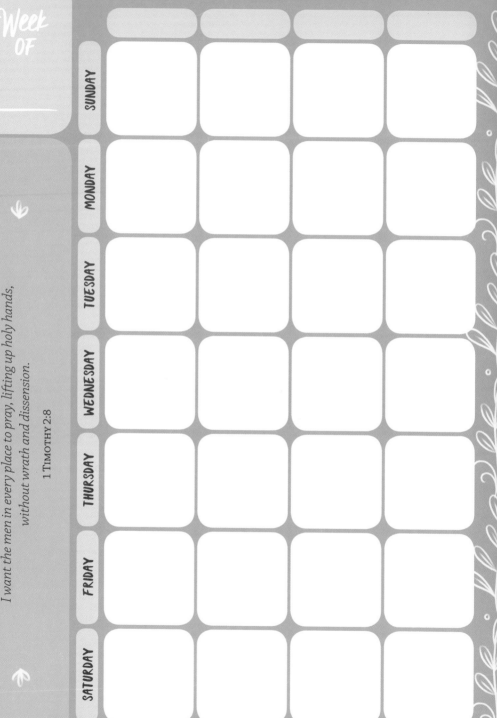

Week
OF
_____

I want the men in every place to pray, lifting up holy hands, without wrath and dissension.

1 TIMOTHY 2:8

SUNDAY

MONDAY

TUESDAY

WEDNESDAY

THURSDAY

FRIDAY

SATURDAY

Week of

_____

Lead me in Your truth and teach me,
for You are the God of my salvation; for You I wait all the day.

PSALM 25:5

	SUNDAY	MONDAY	TUESDAY	WEDNESDAY	THURSDAY	FRIDAY	SATURDAY

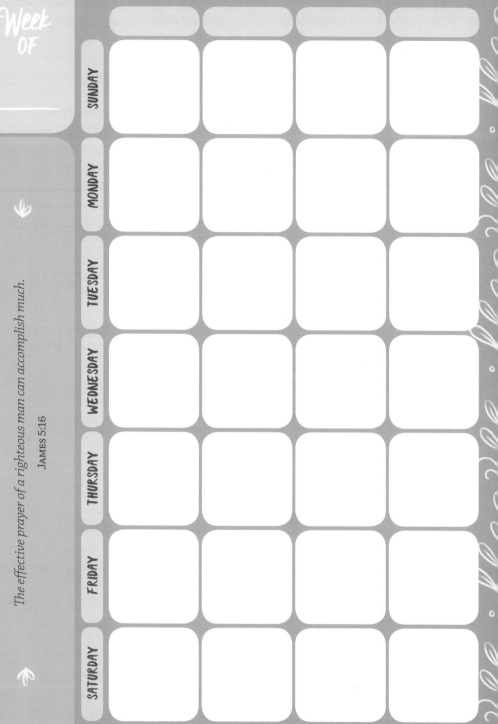

Week OF
_____

The effective prayer of a righteous man can accomplish much.

JAMES 5:16

SUNDAY

MONDAY

TUESDAY

WEDNESDAY

THURSDAY

FRIDAY

SATURDAY

*Those who know Your name will put their trust in You, for You,
O LORD, have not forsaken those who seek you.*

PSALM 9:10

SUNDAY				
MONDAY				
TUESDAY				
WEDNESDAY				
THURSDAY				
FRIDAY				
SATURDAY				

Week of

_____

Answer me when I call, O God of my righteousness!
You have relieved me in my distress; be gracious to me and hear my prayer.

Psalm 4:1

SUNDAY	MONDAY	TUESDAY	WEDNESDAY	THURSDAY	FRIDAY	SATURDAY

Week of

_____

Give ear to my words, O LORD, consider my groaning.
Heed the sound of my cry for help, my King and my God, for to You I pray.

PSALM 5:1-2

	SUNDAY	MONDAY	TUESDAY	WEDNESDAY	THURSDAY	FRIDAY	SATURDAY

Week OF

_____

In the morning, O LORD, You will hear my voice; in the morning
I will order my prayer to You and eagerly watch.

PSALM 5:3

SUNDAY	MONDAY	TUESDAY	WEDNESDAY	THURSDAY	FRIDAY	SATURDAY

Week of

_____

O LORD, the God of my salvation, I have cried out by day and in the night before You.
Let my prayer come before You; incline Your ear to my cry!

PSALM 88:1-2

	SUNDAY	MONDAY	TUESDAY	WEDNESDAY	THURSDAY	FRIDAY	SATURDAY

Week OF

_____

SUNDAY	MONDAY	TUESDAY	WEDNESDAY	THURSDAY	FRIDAY	SATURDAY

God is our refuge and strength, a very present help in trouble. Therefore we will not fear, though the earth should change and though the mountains slip into the heart of the sea.

PSALM 46:1-2

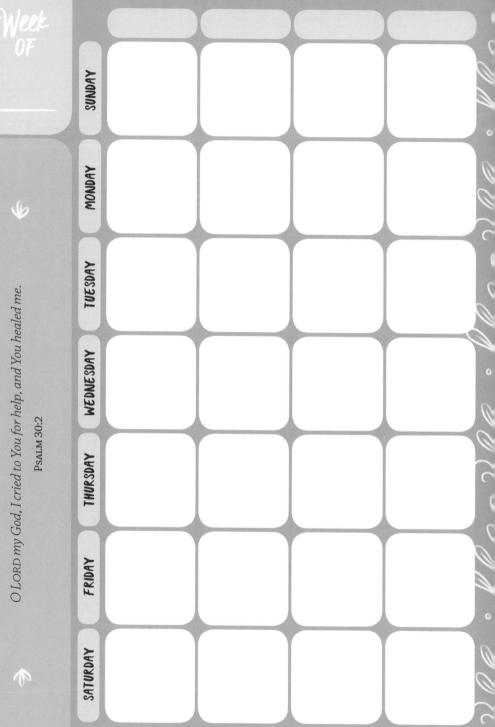

Week OF

_____

O LORD my God, I cried to You for help, and You healed me.

PSALM 30:2

SUNDAY				
MONDAY				
TUESDAY				
WEDNESDAY				
THURSDAY				
FRIDAY				
SATURDAY				

Week OF

_____

SATURDAY · FRIDAY · THURSDAY · WEDNESDAY · TUESDAY · MONDAY · SUNDAY

O God, You are my God; I shall seek You earnestly; my soul thirsts for You, my flesh yearns for You, in a dry and weary land where there is no water.

PSALM 63:1

Week OF

_____

Our help is in the name of the LORD, who made heaven and earth.

PSALM 124:8

	SUNDAY	MONDAY	TUESDAY	WEDNESDAY	THURSDAY	FRIDAY	SATURDAY

Week OF

_____

SUNDAY

MONDAY

TUESDAY

WEDNESDAY

THURSDAY

FRIDAY

SATURDAY

_My soul waits in silence for God only;
from Him is my salvation._

PSALM 62:1

Week OF

_____

SUNDAY

MONDAY

TUESDAY

WEDNESDAY

THURSDAY

FRIDAY

SATURDAY

Seek the LORD and His strength; seek His face continually.
Remember His wonders which He has done, His marvels and the judgments uttered by His mouth.

PSALM 105:4-5

Week of
_____

SUNDAY

MONDAY

TUESDAY

WEDNESDAY

THURSDAY

FRIDAY

SATURDAY

Hear my voice according to Your lovingkindness; revive me, O LORD, according to Your ordinances.

PSALM 119:149

Week OF

____

Evening and morning and noon, I will complain and murmur, and He will hear my voice. He will redeem my soul in peace from the battle which is against me, for they are many who strive with me.

PSALM 55:17-18

	SUNDAY	MONDAY	TUESDAY	WEDNESDAY	THURSDAY	FRIDAY	SATURDAY

Week
OF
_____

SUNDAY

MONDAY

TUESDAY

WEDNESDAY

THURSDAY

FRIDAY

SATURDAY

*God will hear and answer them—
even the one who sits enthroned from of old.*

PSALM 55:19

Week OF

_____

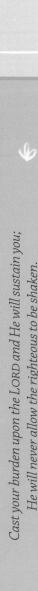

Cast your burden upon the LORD and He will sustain you;
He will never allow the righteous to be shaken.

PSALM 55:22

SUNDAY	MONDAY	TUESDAY	WEDNESDAY	THURSDAY	FRIDAY	SATURDAY

Week
OF
___

SUNDAY

MONDAY

TUESDAY

WEDNESDAY

THURSDAY

FRIDAY

SATURDAY

You have taken account of my wanderings; put my tears in Your bottle.
Are they not in Your book?

PSALM 56:8

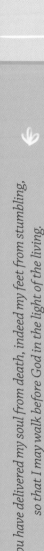

Week OF

_____

You have delivered my soul from death, indeed my feet from stumbling, so that I may walk before God in the light of the living.

PSALM 56:13

SUNDAY				
MONDAY				
TUESDAY				
WEDNESDAY				
THURSDAY				
FRIDAY				
SATURDAY				

Week of

____

SUNDAY

MONDAY

TUESDAY

WEDNESDAY

THURSDAY

FRIDAY

SATURDAY

Week OF

_____

Give ear to my prayer, O God;
and do not hide Yourself from my supplication.

PSALM 55:1

SUNDAY

MONDAY

TUESDAY

WEDNESDAY

THURSDAY

FRIDAY

SATURDAY

Week OF

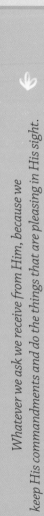

SUNDAY

MONDAY

TUESDAY

WEDNESDAY

THURSDAY

FRIDAY

SATURDAY

Whatever we ask we receive from Him, because we keep His commandments and do the things that are pleasing in His sight.

1 JOHN 3:22

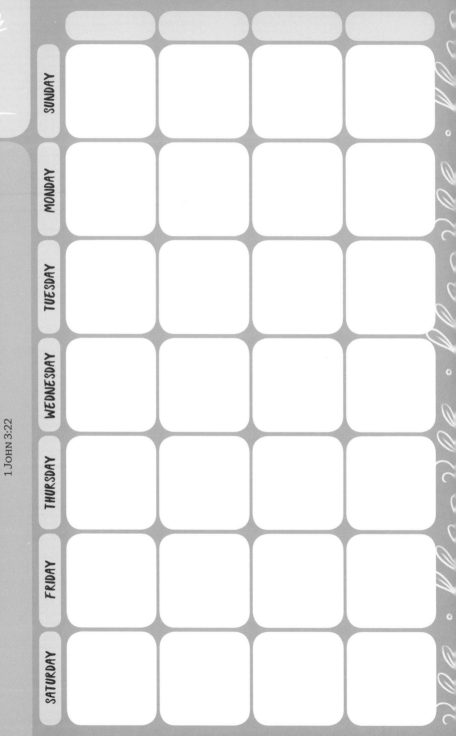

The LORD will command His lovingkindness in the daytime;
and His song will be with me in the night, a prayer to the God of my life.

PSALM 42:8

SUNDAY

MONDAY

TUESDAY

WEDNESDAY

THURSDAY

FRIDAY

SATURDAY

Week
OF

_____

SUNDAY
MONDAY
TUESDAY
WEDNESDAY
THURSDAY
FRIDAY
SATURDAY

Why are you in despair, O my soul? And why are you disturbed within me?
Hope in God, for I shall again praise Him, the help of my countenance and my God.

PSALM 43:5

Week
OF

SUNDAY

MONDAY

TUESDAY

WEDNESDAY

THURSDAY

FRIDAY

SATURDAY

O clap your hands, all peoples; shout to God with the voice of joy.
For the LORD Most High is to be feared, a great King over all the earth.

PSALM 47:1-2

Week OF

_____

Be anxious for nothing, but in everything by prayer and supplication with thanksgiving let your requests be made known to God. And the peace of God, which surpasses all comprehension, will guard your hearts and your minds in Christ Jesus.

PHILIPPIANS 4:6-7

	SUNDAY	MONDAY	TUESDAY	WEDNESDAY	THURSDAY	FRIDAY	SATURDAY

Meditations, Notes, and Prayers

*Let the words of my mouth
and the meditation of my heart
be acceptable in Your sight,
O LORD, my rock and my Redeemer.*

PSALM 19:14

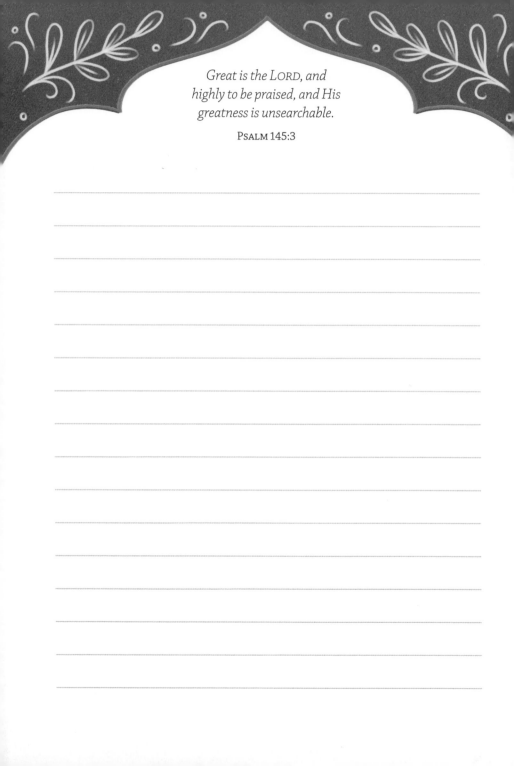

*Great is the LORD, and
highly to be praised, and His
greatness is unsearchable.*

PSALM 145:3

The LORD is gracious and merciful; slow to anger and great in lovingkindness.

PSALM 145:8

*The LORD is good to all,
and His mercies are over
all His works.*

PSALM 145:9

*Be strong and
let your heart take courage,
all you who hope in the LORD.*

PSALM 31:24

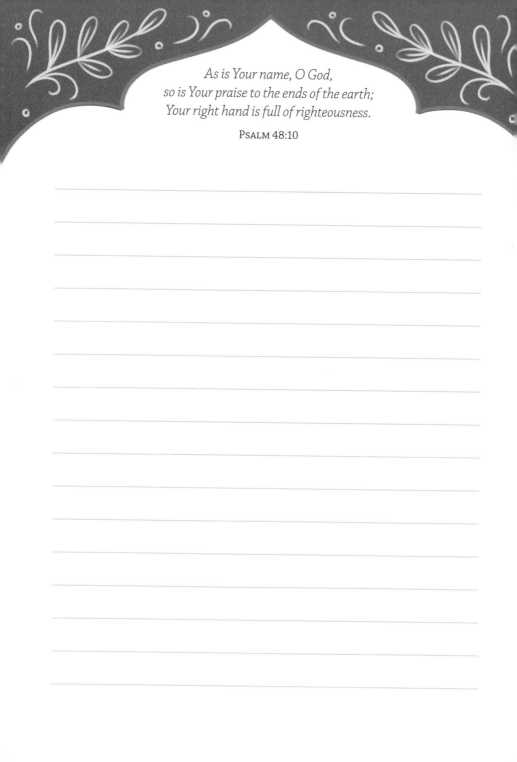

*As is Your name, O God,
so is Your praise to the ends of the earth;
Your right hand is full of righteousness.*

PSALM 48:10

Gracious is the LORD, and righteous;
yes, our God is compassionate.

PSALM 116:5

*The LORD preserves the simple;
I was brought low, and He saved me.*

PSALM 116:6

Return to your rest,
O my soul, for the LORD
has dealt bountifully with you.

PSALM 116:7

*I shall lift up the cup of salvation
and call upon the name of the LORD.*

PSALM 116:13

Hear my cry, O God;
give heed to my prayer.

PSALM 61:1

*He who dwells
in the shelter of the Most High will
abide in the shadow of the Almighty.*

PSALM 91:1

To You I lift up my eyes, O You who are enthroned in the heavens!

PSALM 123:1

Because Your lovingkindness is better than life, my lips will praise You.

PSALM 63:3

*The LORD has done
great things for us; we are glad.*

PSALM 126:3

Those who sow in tears
shall reap with joyful shouting.

PSALM 126:5

The grass withers, the flower fades,
but the word of our God stands forever.

ISAIAH 40:8

My soul, wait in silence
for God only, for my hope is from Him.

PSALM 62:5

He only is my rock and my salvation,
my stronghold; I shall not be shaken.

PSALM 62:6

Let my meditation be pleasing to Him;
as for me, I shall be glad in the LORD.

PSALM 104:34

Hear, O LORD, and be gracious to me; O LORD, be my helper.

PSALM 30:10

*I cried to You; save me
and I shall keep Your testimonies.*

PSALM 119:146

*I rise before dawn and
cry for help; I wait for Your words.*

PSALM 119:147

My eyes anticipate the night watches,
that I may meditate on Your word.

PSALM 119:148

*You are near, O Lord,
and all Your commandments are truth.*

PSALM 119:151

Give thanks to the LORD, for He is good;
for His lovingkindness is everlasting.

PSALM 118:29

O God, hasten to deliver me;
O LORD, hasten to my help!

PSALM 70:1

*Look upon my affliction and
rescue me, for I do not forget Your law.*

PSALM 119:153

Heed the sound of my cry for help,
my King and my God, for to You I pray.

PSALM 5:2

Hear my prayer, O God;
give ear to the words of my mouth.

PSALM 54:2

Help us, O God of our salvation,
for the glory of Your name; and deliver us
and forgive our sins for Your name's sake.

PSALM 79:9

About the Author

Debbie Taylor Williams is the author of seven books and a national keynote Bible teacher and speaker. Her P.R.A.Y. with Passion Across the Nation conference has been held in more than 35 states and simulcast internationally. Best known for her joy and passion for Christ, she gives readers and audiences takeaways to use in everyday life. She and her college sweetheart, Keith, live in the beautiful Texas hill country and are blessed with two children and five grandchildren. When Debbie's not writing or teaching, you'll find her enjoying family and friends, reading, golfing, hiking, traveling, or fishing.

Debbie would love to encourage you with your journaling and faith walk. Get her free *365 Days of Praise* blog. Listen to or watch her journaling podcast tips. Invite her to hold a prayer journaling conference or speak at your event. Find her at:

Website: debbietaylorwilliams.com

Phone: 888.815.9412 or 830.377.2704 (cell)

Email: debbie@debbietaylorwilliams.com

Twitter: @debbietwilliams

Facebook: facebook.com/DebbieTaylorWilliamsAuthor.Speaker/

LinkedIn: linkedin.com/in/debbietaylorwilliams/

Pinterest: pinterest.com/dtwpintrest/